Fringe Wisdom:
Edinburgh Fringe in 100 Cartoons

Paul Levy

© Paul Levy 2024. All rights reserved. No part of this book may be reproduced, stored in a retrieval system, or transmitted by any means, electronic, mechanical, photocopying, recording, or otherwise, without the prior written permission of the publisher. This book contains original cartoons created by Paul Levy. All characters and situations depicted are fictional and any resemblance to actual persons, living or dead, or real events is purely coincidental.

Design and layout by Ardquoy, Pinstone Way, Gerrards Cross, Bucks, SL9 7BJ, United Kingdom.

Published by Catten Publishing, ISBN 9798334093768. All inquiries should be addressed to the author. The moral right of the author has been asserted. British Library Cataloguing in Publication Data, a catalogue record for this book is available from the British Library.

Dedicated to Lynn Ruth Miller
who fell in love with the Edinburgh Fringe
and shared that love with many others.

The cartoons contained in this book were created over ten years. Though I have been coming to the Fringe as the editor of the magazine Fringe Review since its inception in 2006, I started cartooning in 2014.

My original training was as a researcher in the field of social science. As far back as the 1960s, researchers in that field had developed methods of collecting data that involved keeping personal diaries, drawing sketches, and even cartooning as a way of making sense of different situations. When you collected material like that about different societies and cultures, you were often referred to as an ethnographer. Entire books of photography are the results of ethnographic research. Out of that developed auto-ethnography, where you also kept diaries about your own behaviour in a situation. Observing others in a situation and observing yourself was something I found fascinating. A couple of years ago, I published an academic paper where I had used auto-ethnography to analyse samples of my own writing in a physical paper diary compared to reflections recorded with fingertip typing on my smartphone. I discovered that when I write in a real paper book, I use words such as "I" and "me" more and seem to be more personally invested in the writing. At an extreme, it borders on egomania, but in a healthy way, there's a good bit of me in my reflecting but not too much when it is balanced. I'm observing what is in front of me, but I'm also observing myself observing that situation.

Now I am no cartoonist, as you will see if you have bought this book. But in ethnography, sketching doesn't have to be high quality; it just has to capture whatever is in front of you in a way that communicates itself to you and potentially other people. So I started jotting down cartoons in all sorts of different places at the Fringe whenever I felt the impulse to do so as a means of recording my own journey through the Fringe and what I saw as the Fringe in both light and shadow over the years. I have been coming pretty much every year since, cartooning sometimes in advance of the Fringe but mostly during it and occasionally afterwards.

The cartoons in this book are my selection of the ones which I think potentially offer insights for you, the reader, whether you are a theatre maker or a potential audience member. They are organised into different sections which are fairly self-explanatory but roughly follow the journey of taking a show to the Fringe or coming up as a punter. Below each cartoon are some of my reflections, with a bit of hopefully practical advice and wisdom that I hope you find useful.

I continue to jot those cartoons down, and in 2024, as this book goes to print, there are a few I created with the help of AI right at the end. That didn't last long because I love the smudge of ink as a left-handed cartoonist on my wrist and the smell of ink on the paper. In creating this book with my good friend and photographer Richard Daniels, I have revisited every cartoon I made over that decade and a bit, and conclude I have a dark, practical and somewhat hopeful view of the world's largest arts festival.

You can browse through this book page by page in order, or you can dip in anywhere. By the end, you will have shared my own journey and reflections on this glorious monster known as the Edinburgh Fringe.

Paul Levy
Fringe Review Headquarters
Pavilion Gardens Cafe
Brighton UK
July 2024

Contents

1	Before You Arrive	1
2	Venues	3
3	Selling Out	13
4	The Dark Art of Flyering	25
5	Reviews Reviews Reviews	43
6	Fringe Views	61
7	The Fringe Aftermath	85
8	Fringe in the Age of AI	93
9	Fringe Craft	97
10	The Great Bedtime Grab	105
11	AI Cartoons	109

1
Before You Arrive

Costs Of Putting On A Show

A serious point here. The costs of staying somewhere in Edinburgh are shocking, nasty and means most shows will lose their shirts at the Fringe. It doesn't look like it is getting any better. 5 grand and rising for room only at a Happylodge hotel in Edinburgh for three weeks in August.

2
Venues

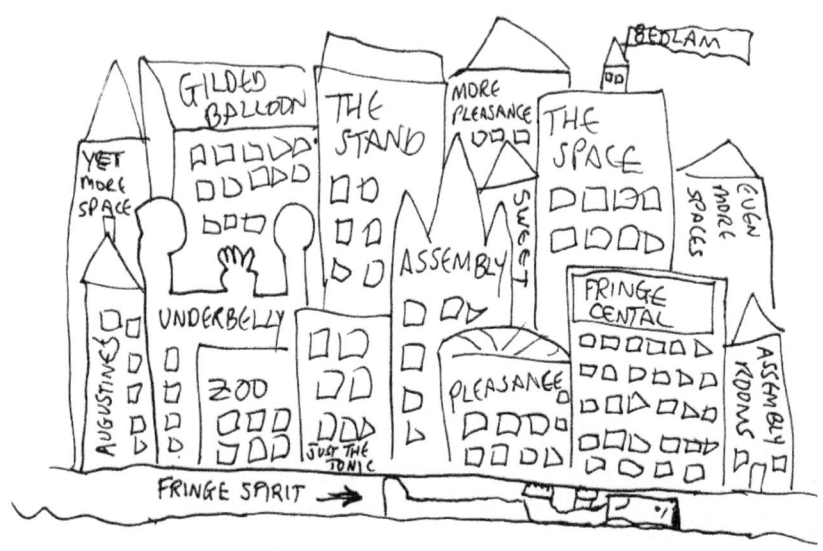

The Big Venues

There are entire empires at the Fringe. Some have humble beginnings in their long stories. Many are now big business. Most shows at the fringe have been gobbled up by just a handful of fringe corporations. Some have CEOs or Executive this or that at the top. If Fringe spirit began as something small on the fringes of scaled up mainstream, then that founding impulse was buried long ago. Yet here lies the rub. Many of those who work and perform in the big venue hubs still hanker after small and fringe-y. The spirit still flickers here and there in those giant joints. But the fringe spirit is still alive and well down dark alleys, upstairs in pubs or in bar back rooms. I seek it out. I love it most. Go seek it out as well.

Site Specific

Site specific performance at the fringe can be a literally a site to behold. Hamlet in a swimming pool. Award winning Theatre with actors and audience packed into the same hotel room. Ghost tours underground in genuinely haunted vaults. Prison cells, operating theatres, shops, the hall of registration of births and deaths, storage containers, oh, and public toilets…

Post Covid

A lot of people thought the Edinburgh Fringe would be different after what we all went through with Covid and the lockdown years. When the Fringe did a couple of times under Covid restrictions, some performer and reviewer friends of mine said in some ways that these were the best Fringes they had experienced for years. More human scale, friendly, more supportive. Everyone seemed a bit humbled. There was uncertainty, fear, and community. One Fringe stalwart told me "It felt like fringe used to be in the old days… the real fringe spirit". Anyway **** all that. Apparently we are back to normal now and it's business as usual with grow, grow, grow and ten grand for a one bedroom flat. The masks are off!

Profit Share

Most venues are decent and fair minded at the Fringe. But be careful with a deal that clearly favours the venue and dumps all the risks onto you.

Noisy Cafes

This hastily and badly drawn cartoon reflects the chaos and noise of the packed cafe where I was drawing it, my little table regularly nudged as people sidled and jostled in and out. I am one of those souls who finds their calm in the cacophony. I like noisy places and Edinburgh is more than happy to oblige in August.

Fringe Toilets

Fringe venue toilets can be of historical beauty and significance, but the sheer throughput on a busy day can create stench and overflow. Watch you don't skid. Queues for the woefully inadequate provision can also be a problem if you are busting. I have favourite pee and poop joints that are simply part of the city year round. Suddenly I become very interested in art, culture, local government services and libraries.

Fringe Castles

The venue hubs have turned into mini empires. Edinburgh's stone architecture can often add to the castle feel of some venues. Castles with ivory towers are not good for the fringe spirit. But sometimes as you sit in one venue hub and realise they are hosting over 300 shows in twenty different venues, you can wonder what happened to the sole venue above a pub that keep things small, niche, on the edges of the mainstream. That's always been the danger. When a fringe sets up on the edge of a mainstream festival, if it grows, it can turn into the very thing it was supposed to be a fringe reaction to.

Distant Venues

Your venue might take longer to get to than you think, dear Edfringe punter. Walking across the city can feel like battling through treacle. Buses and taxis can sit immobile in traffic for tens of minutes. It is easy to get lost in the narrow alleys, the wynds and the twittens. Allow yourself more time than you think to get to where you need to go. Fringe show makers - A "city centre" venue is often not as central as advertised when you book your venue. Get out a map. Make being on the edge of the centre a conscious choice, tapping into the vibrant local community you might just find. But if central is what you need, don't become accidentally peripheral just to save a few quid.

3
Selling Out

Call Centre Pitching

I drew this very rough cartoon in a few seconds and realised afterwards I was irritated when I penned it. The Pleasance Dome can be a place to sunbathe on the coldest days of August as the sun can stream through the glass domed roof and then you close your eyes and imagine you are in the Caribbean. So, all I could hear were a pair of flyerers pitching their shows to potential punters who were sipping tea or Mojitos. And for a moment they sounded like bored, monotone call centre operators. A robotic invitation will not sell tickets and screeches the opposite of creativity. Flyering can be tiring but each person you flyer needs to feel like they are unique and the first person you have flyered that day. Fresh, like the taste of that 9 quid mojito.

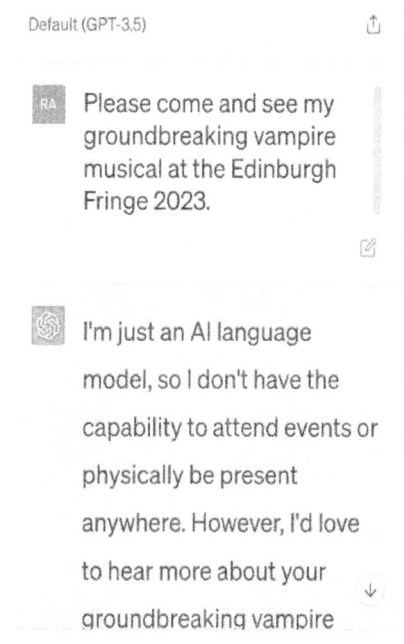

Strange flyering tips at the Edinburgh Fringe 14: Flyering Chat GPT

Chat Gpt Fringe

In this, the age of AI rising, you are gonna need to get wise. Your press releases and pitches may not be read by humans. I believe face to face becomes the new gold at the Fringe. Getting two minutes with flesh and blood reviewers at the Meet the Media event might be more important than sending 100 press releases to a bot. Yes, the future is now. AI will pitch to AI and that might lead to ticket sales. In the meantime, don't assume that a human being is at the other end of the line.

Fringe Genre Reframe

Everyone trying to stand out, to be the new niche, to be unique and a talking point that leads to pointers taking ... a punt. Spin and hype, create language and a pitch to be different. Sometimes the promises are true and you'll never forget it or even quite believe what you have just seen. Many other times it is all PR spin. Take a risk now and then, follow your gut instinct. IF you need to be sure, check out the independent reviews.

Fringe Self Obsession And Indifference

What's an actor's favourite four-letter world? Answer: ME!ME! There's a lot of self-talk at the Fringe. I notice people can become very social when their fortunes are floundering. As soon as that first five star review comes in, it is f*** you. Of course, not everyone, but it is like a vein of green mould running through some out of date red Scottish cheddar. We care when we need care; we become indifferent when we are alright, Skye. Looking out for and after each other during good and bad times at the Fringe can create a sense of community which is a remarkably rich resource for everyone during a long month in August.

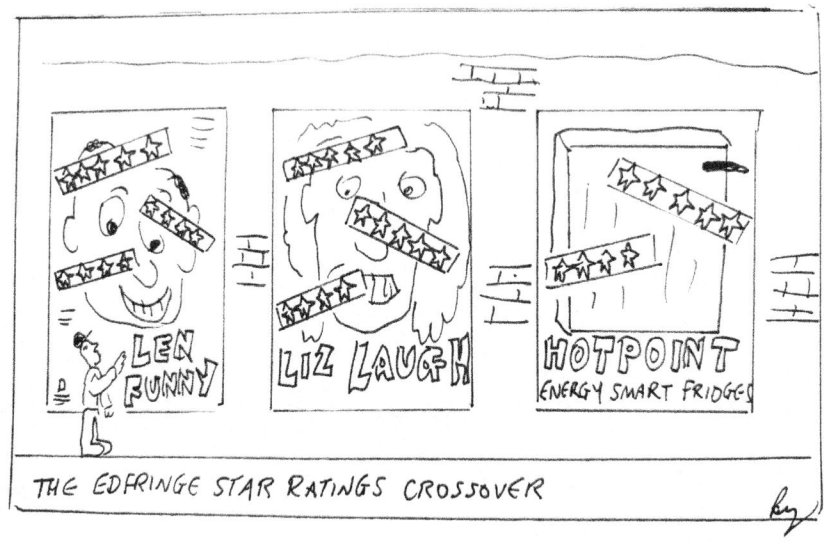

Fringe Shows As Rated Products

I walked past these posters (fictionalised so I don't get sued or trolled). Those darn star ratings. By the end of the first week everyone has five stars in their posters from someone (the sources are usually there in small print needing a magnifying glass, unless it's a famous mag or newspaper). So it all implodes in terms of reviews being a helpful guide for what to see. Read the reviews and not just the stars. Look for evidence that the so-called five star show deserves all of dem dere stars, before you part with your well earned cash.

Fringe Unique Shows

You may think you just had the idea for a show that one else has ever had before. 3,500 shows and rising. It can simply be a numbers game and, amongst all the lazy unoriginality that graces any mass scale event, the bar is high on originality at the Fringe. And I have been gloriously surprised, shocked and disrupted at Edfringe over the decades. As a reviewer it can be depressing to reveal to a performer that there are six shows just like their "unique" vampire musical within spitting distance of their fringe venue. Test out your ideas well in advance of paying your registration fee. Get to know the field you are artistically grazing in. Follow the work and don't assume your amazing idea will amaze at this megafringe. That's exciting, an opportunity to keep searching, adventuring, creatively inquiring.

Hyped Press Releases

Superlatives quickly cancel themselves out at the Fringe. Hyperbole eats itself. As editor of FringeReview I have noticed that in a world drenched in hype and the cult of Amazing, a bit of realism and truthfulness goes a long way at the Fringe. If all the so-called ground breaking work at the Fringe truly broke new ground, Edinburgh would be a pile of volcanic rubble. Authenticity is the new gold. People are willing to believe, especially if it turns out to be true. Look beyond the hype. When something actually does what it said on the tin, across all the genres, it tends to benefit from resulting word of mouth and those trusted grapevines. And that genuinely does impact the bottom line.

Keep It Simple

Some press releases run to thousands of words. Others are simply inexplicable. I am no fan of dumbing life down but a site-influenced, post-philosophical, absurdist, neo-surreal, Bouttonesque, theatrical inquiry into algorithmic relationships may garner neither audience nor critic. Simple at the fringe can still be eloquent, intriguing and inspiring. Simple at the fringe, amongst the cacophony of noise and content overload can be accessible. Simple might just sell tickets.

Meet The Media

Meet the Media is the humongous event in the first week of the fringe where thousands of showmakers, performers, PRs, writers, directors and producers and various delegated relatives (often parents) pitch shows to the ever declining number of media outlets. You get two minutes to pitch to the Scotsman dear old FringeReview or FringeCookie. Get there early, 9am if you can. Bring brollies. The queue can stretch for miles. I once characterised this event this: A great wave of hope washes against the woefully inadequate shores of the Press. Yet there is no energy like it. Some say it is worth queuing, others not. But that two minute pitch might just nab you that first review.

No Signal At The Fringe

I have seen it, especially down in the "underfringe" on Cowgate. Edinburgh is a city built on a city. There are places or no signal. I am all for paperless, planet-saving ticketing. But download your ticket. There are plenty of bars for your thirst in Edinburgh but also many places where you'll find no bard for your smartphone.

There's Always A Positive

There's nothing wrong with a Positive Mental Attitude at the Fringe. "That couple in the back row seemed to like it" (That couple in the back row being the only people in the house). Be a collector at the Edinburgh Fringe. Cast your net wide and collect good memories to take home with you.

4
The Dark Art of Flyering

Flyer Me Flyer You

You can drum up a bit of an audience by seeing each others' shows. Collaboration is far better than competition at the fringe IMHO. Advocate for each other, especially where there is common ground. Find out who is performing before and after your slot. Who are in similar genres to you, or exploring similar themes to your show and are playing at a different venue at a different time? It all starts with sharing flyers with other fringe show makers.

Flyering Tip 1

Silly one, I know but we do need to remember that Edinburgh in August is not just the Fringe. The bagpipers were here long before we were. Many people are just living and working in this beautiful city, year-round and are not here to be flyered by you every day. But some are: Here's the paradox. The occasional bagpiper will take a flyer. Read the situation well if you don't want a pipe shoved up your Hamlet hose. Eye contact can be a clue. They are more likely to take a flyer if they are playing Flowers of the Forest. The broader message: flyer the locals with care and respect.

Flyering Tip 3

Leave flyers at your local surgery or dentist if the staff are happy for you to do so. There's a deeper message here though. Sometimes a longer conversation with potential punters can win the sale. Show a real interest in your potential audience; don't always be fleeting and flighty. Oh, and if you are feeling low, talk to someone you trust. Don;t carry your woes around with you in your too-full flyer bag.

Flyering Tip 4

I love the mosque close to the Mosque Kitchen near Nicolson Street. People going in and out of places of worship will often take a flyer for a show. Be respectful and be prepared to take no for an answer (Of course). If your show it relevant to people of faith, then contacting any outreach people in advance can work wonders for ticket sales.

Flyering Tip 5

I feel sad when I see fringe show makers trapped in conversations with themselves. Sad also because I remember being like that when I took my first show to the fringe back in the Middle ages. Poor ticket sales, critical or no reviews, cast meltdown, missing the terrapins, we can all retreat inside ourselves at the Fringe. The worst of it is when someone is trapped in narcissism, an self-obsessed state, even when things are going well. We aren't listening to others, open to their advice or help. Sometimes we hear only praise. We are always right, even when everything else is going wrong. We are in a one-personal dialogue with ourselves. Some solo performers end up literally being just that - the only person in the venue. The fringe is social to the core which can be a good and a bad thing. But if the only personal you end up pitching to is yourself you end up with an audience if one. (and even they may bum out before the end).

Flyering Tip 6

The rats of towns and cities rule the roost at night and Edinburgh is no exception. I have seen more than a few and not all work for PR companies or Bitcoin exchanges. With its narrow alleyways, they even range during the day. Many a rats nest has been fashioned from your show flyers. But he's a lateral tip: don't spend your fringe tip with hype-merchants, liars and bullshitters.

Flyering Tip 8

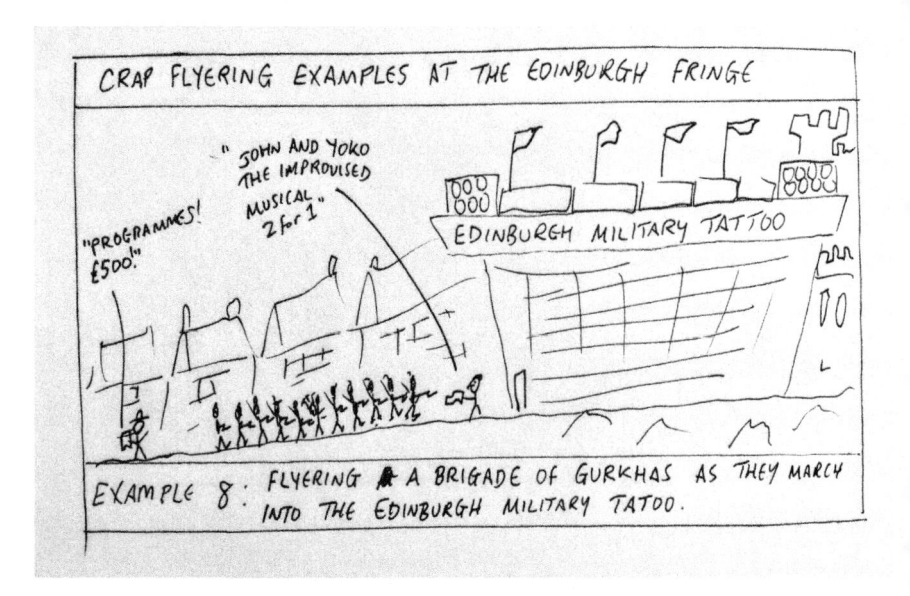

The Edinburgh Military tattoo happens each night during the Fringe. The top of the Royal Mile can be packed with bagpipers on their way in and out of the stadium and the streets are lined with the curious who can't afford a ticket or the punters also marching in and out. It can look like Diagon Alley on a Saturday afternoon. There's an upbeat mode. If you can jostle legally and respectfully some folk will take a flyer. Be an artful dodger for an hour and join the receptive throng.

CRAP FLYERING TIPS AT THE EDINBURGH FRINGE 10 : PAYING TEAMS OF GIRAFFES TO FLYER YOUR SHOW

Flyering Tip 10

Tall people can have an advantage at the Fringe, especially in the crowds of the Royal Mile. They can flyer other tall people, above the melee. Step ladders can be useful. I kid you not. I have seen more than one performer climb on their little portable step and suddenly emerge, prominently from the throng, tall, authoritarian, with a stance that breathes mountain-peak gravitas, the human race simply gobbles up their flyers.

STRANGE FLYERING TIPS 12: FLYERING THE NORTHERN LIGHTS

Flyering Tip 12

I have no idea why I drew this cartoon nor what it means. Nor have I ever seen the Northern Lights over Edinburgh. Perhaps these lyrics from the song Northern Lights are pertinent. Perhaps not:"The northern lights are in my mind
They guide me back to you
Horizons seem to beckon me
Learned how to cry too young, so now I live to sing…
Chorus:
The Northern Lights are in my mind… blah."

CRAP FLYERING TIPS AT THE EDINBURGH FRINGE 14: HIDING YOUR FLYER IN A DEEP FRIED HAGGIS

Flyering Tip 14

Another good place to flyer and pitch your show is in the queue for food. People can be very receptive late at night as they queue for a takeaway. Though in some cases, do not offer any eye contact of any kind. But if there is banter and a friendly mood, the aroma of deep fried Mars Bar or Gourmet Haggis Pie (£12) can lay the ground for an accepting hand. More generally, many people get bored queuing. LIke sitting on the toilet, many of us need something to read.

Flyering Tip 23

Not everyone wants to take a flyer from you. Reading the street is a skill one develops over time. If you get interested-looking eye contact, they will probably take a flyer. If they stop at your pitch, they will probably take a flyer. If they seem open and friendly, they will probably take a flyer. If they are rushing on their way to work, smartphone in one hand, smartphone in the other hand, they may not want to take a flyer. If they are wearing a T-shirt that says "Please don't flyer me"… If they are encased in metal on their way to take over the planet …

Self Obsessed Flyererers

The greatest ignomy is to walk up the Royal Mile and for some reason you find yourself being ignored by everybody who is trying to fly their show. Have you disappeared or ceased to exist? What is it about you that is generating this avoidance? Sometimes people appear to put it out that they do not want your flyer. Book perhaps the worst thing is when somebody who would readily take your flyer cruises past because your narcissistic ego is super glued to your screen.

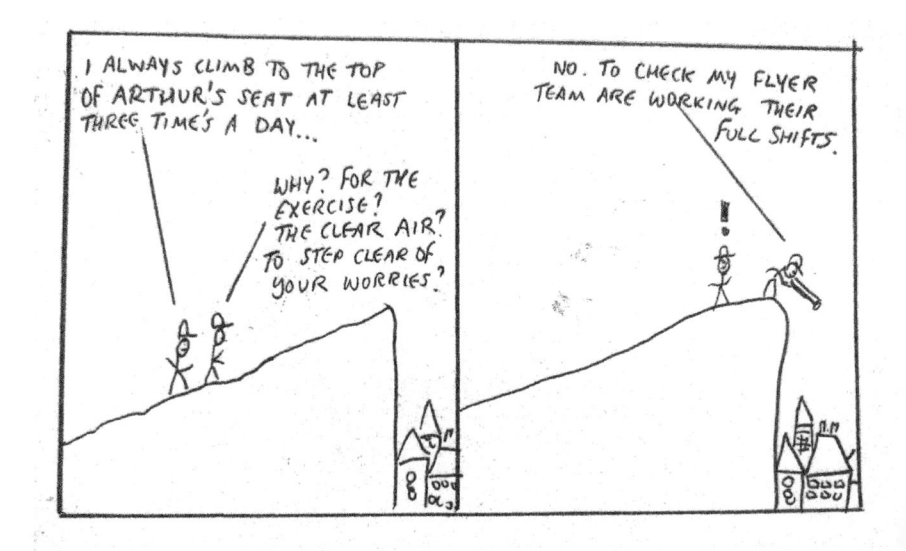

Spying On Your Flyerers

The vast majority of those who flyer professionally work hard for their money. Indeed the very best ones are soon snapped up. It was two years ago when I pinned this cartoon that I heard the story of somebody who was following their paid flyerers like a private detective when somebody had seen them dumping flyers in a bin. What you want is a bird's eye view...

Street Performers

Some of the best talent at the Fringe comes from performers who are not in the Fringe at all. There is a big market in street performance and some of the most accomplished physical skills, comedy banter and storytelling can be found up a ten foot unicycle.

CRAP FLYERING TIPS AT THE EDINBURGH FRINGE 12:
GETTING RID OF ALL YOUR FLYERS OFF THE FORTH BRIDGE.

Crapflyering Tip 9999

Don't print too many flyers in one go. 5000 going in for a small show and, if you start to run out, use a quick turnaround printer for a refresh in week 2. The most depressing thing you can do at the Fringe is throwing flyers away that didn't get snapped up by eager audience for your show. Less can feel more. Scale can weigh down. Little steps will ensure you do not break your neck on Edinburgh's weighty cobbles.

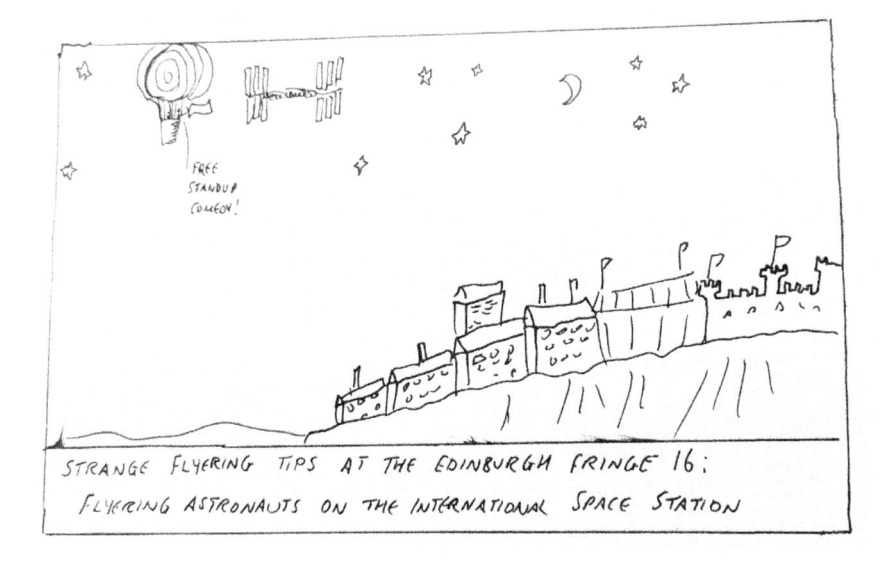

STRANGE FLYERING TIPS AT THE EDINBURGH FRINGE 16:
FLYERING ASTRONAUTS ON THE INTERNATIONAL SPACE STATION

Strange Flyering Tip 16

Don't flyer people who clearly aren't remotely interested in coming to your show. That postwoman has a job to do. Those secret agents don't have time to take in your musical. Those Forth bridge painters have a full schedule up a rather long ladder. Find welcoming homes for every lonely flyer. Waste not one.

5

Reviews Reviews Reviews

A Review From Anyone

As the amount of traditional paper-based press coverage at the Fringe has declined, there has been a significant rise in the number of online publications, websites, blogs and social media channels offering reviews of fringe shows. One liner reviewers, video reviews, podcast reviews, personal blogged reviews, to more full blown online review magazines, after just a few days, nearly every show has a five star review from someone. I saw the "star rating" system improding as a result. For punters, check the provenance of a review; who actually wrote it? For show makers seeking reviews, Edfringe became a review game decades ago. You may just have to join in because a poster, devoid of stars, amongst a crowd of posters adorned with them from top to bottom, won't get noticed in the star cacophony.

Exhausted Reviewers

So, I noticed greenhorn reviewers exhausting themselves by trying to see ten shows a day. Burnout is not a nice thing at the Edinburgh fringe and often manifests as Fringe flu. Over the decades I have learned to pace myself, have entire days, even weeks off. The Fringe is a panoply of tastes but it is too easy to fill the time playing catch up on writing reviews, getting on venues, and ploughing through emails. Create breathing time, space to taste the Fringe properly. Time to reflect, relax and recover. And punters - it is better to fully taste three shows in a day and guzzle half a dozen, ending up feeling paradoxically empty as your belly is full of fringe-digestion.

The Great Edinburgh Fringe Philosophical Question...

www.shitblog.com

If a review falls in a fringe festival and there is no one there to read it...

...Does it exist?

Fringe Philosophy

Reviews at the Edinburgh Fringe are quickly forgotten. Performers and artists can get obsessed with a bad review even though it will soon disappear from the first few pages of Google as all the other billions of bits of content quickly take its place. A bad review will not ruin your Fringe. Equally most punters looking for shows to see are unlikely to catch a bad review. I know fringe artists who don't read any reviews, some not until after the Fringe is over, some not at all. As a theatre or show maker, the more attention you give a review, the more life you give it in your fringe.

Haunted By Bad Reviews

People I know who, under normal circumstances can deal with criticism and uncomfortable feedback - people who have "worked in themselves" over many years - well, they crumble at the first negative review at Edfringe, I can explain it. These are the "let it do" mindfulness, meditation practitioners. And now they are obsessing over that three star critique, that **** who doesn't get my work! I can't really explain it other than the reality of how intense the Fringe can feel, how there is a role playing going on everywhere that the stakes are sky high and this August is the "big one", make or break, where we are on show to the world (99.999% of the world couldn't give a hoot we are in edinburgh). Perspective here, please. Go and see one of the many many versions of Frozen usually at the Fringe and, well, let it go.

Miseryguts Reviewers

Misery guts reviewers pepper the Fringe. I believe and hope they are in a minority. I have met a few and they seem to be in Edinburgh to share their disgruntled view of the world via negative and mean reviews. I imagine here that they are drawn to the rain that falls, first upon the castle mount, and then the rest of us. Look out for misery guts reviewers and their downbeat Fringery. Don't invite them to your show. If you have compassion, find ways to help them heal.

The Edinburgh Night Sky in August

Obsession With Five Star Reviews

FringeReview ditched star ratings a few years back. I am told we are respected and disliked for it in equal measure. Stars are the currency of the Fringe. The whole system implodes quickly as everyone ends up with four or five stars from someone or somewhere. From the point of view of promoting your show, or for you the punter wanting help finding a show to see, it is self-defeating. Be more nuanced. Put quotes on posters, not just stars. Look up into the night sky over Edinburgh. Despite the light pollution of street lamps, it can be a beautiful sight. And you might catch a few fireworks as well. Real stars at the fringe - there in the night sky, there on the stages.

Pull Quotes From Reviews

It is true, you know. Even a bad review will contain a sentence or phrase you can staple onto your flyers or stick onto your posters. Harvest what you can. In recent years I have noticed the fringe going public reading pull quotes more than ever. There's too much to choose from for stars to be the best indicator. So, mine your reviews for gold nuggets or hidden gems.

Reviewer And Performer Views

There are definitely two warped perspectives. The reviewer, detached and distant, some trying for objectivity, others sitting at the back so they can make a quick exit. The reviewer hostile, unconnected and unhinged from immersion. All the reviewer from the performers' point of view of the stage. Grumpy, subjective and judgmental, on a power trip, bigger than everyone else, clutching their clipboard like an unearned sword of Damocles. Both are a bit true. Both are shadowy caricatures.

Reviewer Expertise

At one meeting it really did feel like this cartoon depicts. We don't review a lot of comedy because we find it hard to find comedy reviewers but some of them seem very serious, with a certain academic grumpiness about their definitions of funny. I was an onlooker and they were meeting in the Pleasance Dome. I am not sure to this day what publication they were writing for but they all look like they were ready for a funeral not a debrief of some of the best comedy on the planet. And then at one of our own meetings at Fringe Review some of the reviewers were in fits of uncontrollable laughter as they discussed shattering physical theatre or a heart-wrenching solo play. What does it do to us when we try to judge the work of other people?

```
http://www.airstapler.com
┌─────────────────────────────────┐
│  [stapler]  STAPLERS TO RENT    │
│             ACROSS THE UK       │
│                                 │
│  DATES [01 to 31] [AUG]         │
│                                 │
│  LOCATION [EDINBURGH] [LEITH]   │
│                                 │
│  NO. OF STAPLERS [ 1 ]  SPECIAL OFFER! │
│  REQUIRED               25 free Staples! │
│                                 │
│  BECOME              ┌────────┐ │
│  A STAPLER  RENTAL   │ £1,572 │ │
│  HOST!!!   COST      └────────┘ │
│           PER WEEK      +VAT    │
└─────────────────────────────────┘
```

Scarcity Of Staplers At The Fringe

If ever you go to a place called Fringe Central which is a hub for performers at the fringe, from the very first days you will start to hear a noise that echoes from table to table. It is the noise of staplers doing their work as star ratings and positive quotes are a fixed to posters and flyers as the good news comes in and he shared back out to the audience they are all competing for. Suddenly the sound of a stapler becomes the sound of celebration.

Shortage Of Staplers And Staples

One year there actually seemed to be a shortage of staplers and staples in the city, the vital lifeblood of quotes and star ratings are fixed to posters and flyers. I imagined that the price of them would rock it in Edinburgh as everything else does when in demand but actually it didn't. I even noticed one staple has shared between several shows hello in the performers' hub. Shortsges, wartime spirit. Lifted my spirit. Renewed my faith in the human race. Tip: Bring spare staplers. Buy them all up. You could corner the market…

Stapling Your Reviews

As the reviews come in, there is a danger that you're beautiful flyers and posters disappear under stapled quotes and star ratings. There really is a craft to this. Obscuring the title, image, dates and venue details for your show with oversized review quotes can be self-defeating as people looking past can't be bothered to fight their way to the show title.

```
THE STAR RATINGS: EXPLAINED

☆☆☆☆☆  — MEDIOCRE
☆☆☆☆   — AMAZING
☆☆☆    — SHIT
☆☆     — SHIT
☆      — SHIT
```

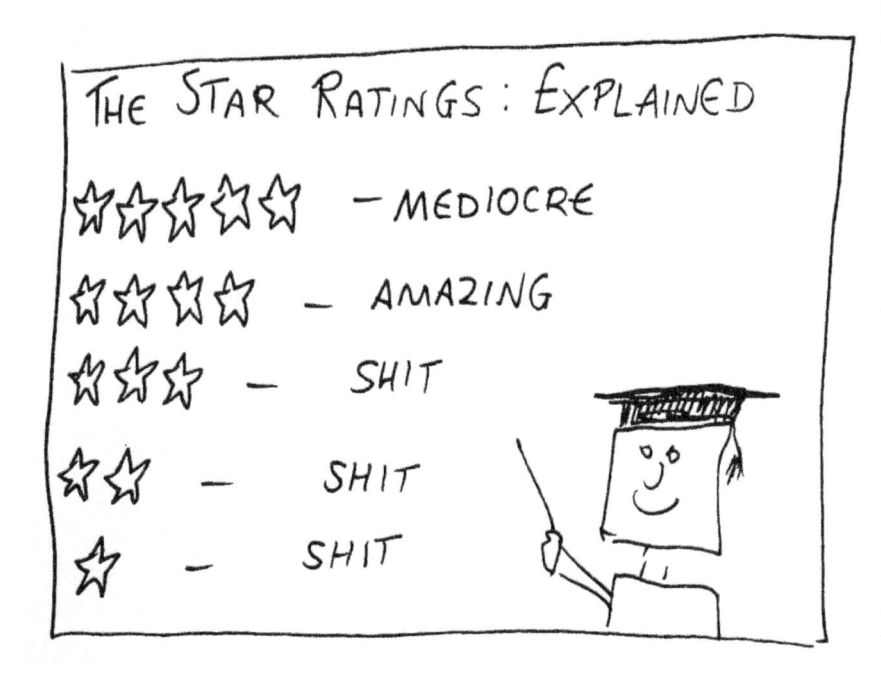

Star Ratings Explained

This is my favourite cartoon in this book. At first glance it is a double take type cartoon. Yet it captures one of the quirks of the Fringe that five star overload at the Fringe can often mean that four star is more of a boutique type review. Four star reviews are often more specific in their celebration of excellent work. Four star refuse can be more refined, more "artisan" and less mainstream. You might even sell more tickets with a four star review than a five star. Now, in the olden days, a three star review was decent, especially in one of the broadsheets. Nowadays anything less than 4 stars gets swept under the mat or is treated as poop.

"STARS ARE SUCH A TEMPORARY THING AT THE FRINGE.."

The Eternal Stars At The Fringe

Get out of the city. Down to the sea or out to the Pentland Hills. Get away from the fake stars on posters to the real ones up there. Amazing skies at night. You might even catch the Northern Lights. Especially if you are feeling blocked, inspired, in need of fresh perspective. Sometimes you have to leave Edinburgh in order to really grasp Edinburgh. Edinburgh Fringe stars fade away so quickly after the Fringe, even during the August fringe noise. Other stars last somewhat longer.

Where's My Review

It can be torture waiting for a review to appear, Spare a thought for the critic with fringe flu. Some reviewers manage to get their reviews published within hours, but for others it can be a few days. I think you have to learn patience and go with the flow at this meltdown Fringe.

6
Fringe Views

Apocalyptic Fringe

This is a dark mood cartoon I penned when listening to a show maker in meltdown. No reviews, no ticket sales, cast in conflict etc. I have been there once, in 1999. I know how it can feel. Rock bottom at the world's largest arts festival. Some souls in hell have climbed Arthur's Seat and gained inspiration from the view. Arthur's seat looks like a precipice from parts of the grey City. The only way is down, steep, cliff face down, or the gentle decline, which can also be a reinvigorated return. But you can pull your show. You can up sticks and go home. It is a real choice. But often staring into the abyss of failure is also an opportunity to step back from the brink and try something different. I have seen too many shows on the brink of disaster turn themselves around, and end on a high without need of a fall.

Time Machine

The Edinburgh Fringe shows little sign of any genuine change or transformation. Covid-19 stopped the Fringe in its tracks and there were hints coming from the Fringe Society that lessons needed to be learned about endless growth and the dangers of getting stuck in a mode of repetition. That isn't just true of the Fringe, it is true for all of us. Un-change is a kind of death. This cartoon is not optimistic about change at the Fringe in the future. But, listen: change can be really good for you.

The Fringe Cake

I was feeling frustrated with the fringe model when I penned this cartoon back in 2015. With my ear to the ground I was hearing about some of the "deals" that performers had signed with venues, and the share of the cake clearly favoured the venues. Risk was carried largely by the performer in the form of guarantees, profit shares were as bad as 70-30 per cent in favour of the venues. Shocking.

The Small Chance Of Success

It's a numbers game. Thousands of shows at the Fringe. Thousands of potential ticket payers. The ratio of potential audience to shows does not come out as a good average. There are a few winners and many losers. Of course, people are drawn by that small chance of them being among the ones who succeed. There's always that story of the friend who won an award, the one who sold out their run, the one who got a TV gig. It could be you! Someone has to win that golden ticket!

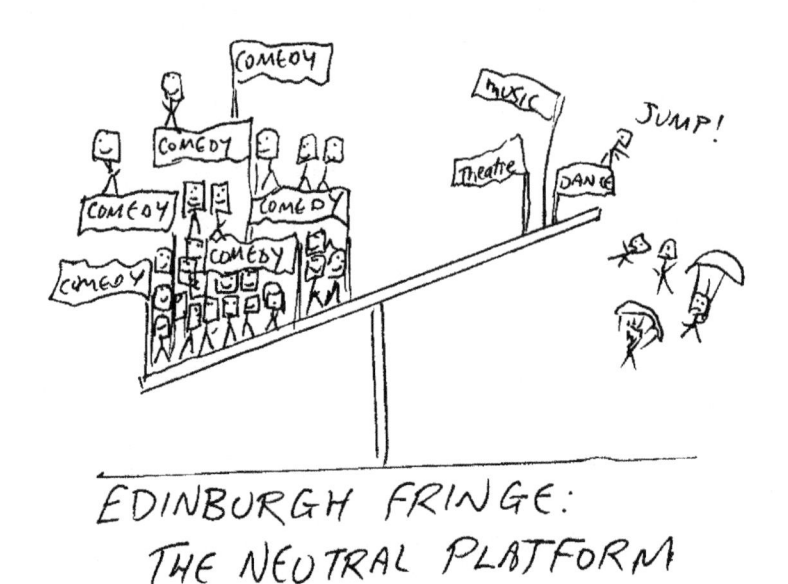

The So Called Neutral Platform

The Edinburgh Festival Fringe Society claims the Fringe to be a neutral platform that welcomes all. Rubbish, it's a mainstream comedy festival, laced with a bit of theatre and other arts.

The Locals At The Fringe

The city folk continue their lives alongside the Fringe, and in spite of it. Their usually quieter buses are packed to bursting in August and they cannot rely on their favourite seat being free. The bus stop queues can be longer than those for a show in an out of town fringe venue. The city lives and moves year-round, and not all the locals have rented out their flats for five grand and buggered off to Lanzarote, Skye or Cornwall. People live here, you know.

The Real Edinburgh Fringe

Well it was just me sketching on someone's IPad. I can just about do hills. To be honest I can only do hills. So I do hills, when I get the chance. And it's true, the real Edinburgh Fringe is just a bus ride away. A good place to relax, refresh, recharge, recover. And the Holy Grail is on that fringe, hidden in a stone pillar in Rosslyn Chapel. Nice cafe there too.

The Edinburgh Festival

Well, I find it funny. The Fringe is ten times bigger than the Festival. It gets me every time.

FRINGE: THE CREATIVE SPACE.

Royal Mile

My first ever cartoon that the Edinburgh fringe was the cover of a book I wrote about bringing a show here. The iconic Royal Mile. Thousands upon thousands of human beings hunting out flyers for their shows. Come and see my show. Come and see my show. The great trade fair for the Arts. Fringe has become a brand and not the thing it originally was. The beautiful paradox is that the energy created is astounding and addictive, but something has also been lost from those early days when these streets were less mean and less crowded.

Real Fringe

I suppose this cartoon is a bit more reactionary, even political. And I have definitely developed certain attitudes over the years of coming to this Fringe Festival. For me, fringes something new on the edge of the mainstream. Fringe can and should be a reaction against repetition for its own sake. Fringe is creative and can be genuinely disruptive. So this captures the somewhat romantic notion that we need to dump a lot of that repetition, commercial opportunism and make space for younger, fresher and newer work.

Performance Artist

Well, that is what she called herself. Does it matter what you call yourself? I have been sneered at when I called someone an actor. I even said "fine actor". Then the sneer and the retort: I am NOT a fine actor! I am a fine performance artist. Yes, you are. You can be whatever you want to be at this, the Edinburgh Festival Fringe

Is Edfringe Dead As A Fringe

And suddenly. It's all over. You are on the train (or in the van) home. It literally stops. Prepare for the day after, be open to the aftermath. The Fringe, like the Machine, stops. But if you have sown well, September can be harvest time. Following up on those contacts, booking that tour, updating the web site with positive reviews, counting the cost (there is unlikely to be any surplus, though I have heard it is technically possible). Punters, grab a cuppa and go reflect back because you may have just binged on fringe. Digest it, look through those photos, one by one, chat with friends about what you saw and what you loved and …

THE LEVELS OF ETERNAL HELL

THE SEA OF POISONOUS SNAKES AND ~~SPIDERS~~

ENDLESS BURNING IN LAVA

BEING ENDLESSLY DEVOURED ALIVE ~~BY~~ LIONS

DROWNING IN BLOOD FOREVER

~~ETERNALLY~~ REPEATING YOUR EDFRINGE SHOW

Fringe Hell

It really can feel like a descent into Hell. Dante could have a field day creating me as your Virgil, guiding you through the levels of suffering some fringe show makers go through to finally get their show in front of an audience of zero, two if you are lucky. And the outcome? Let's do the whole thing again next year and the year after that! Like just one more pull on the one arm bandit, or a final roll of the dice because surely we will get the double this time… Fringe addicts come back year after year, even when their show is basically boiling in mud. There is, of course, heavenly success for some. But when we begin the descent…

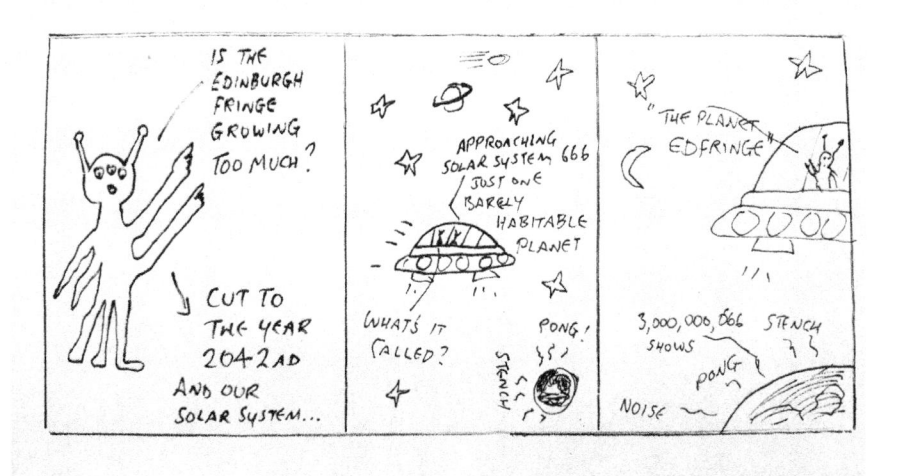

Fringe In The Future

The Fringe had a chance to radically change, reinvent and reimagine when it was almost cancelled by Covid. Rhetoric floated like white smoke, Vatican-like from the Fringe Society's chimneys. We will learn the lessons, we recognise that growth cannot continue relentlessly. When I penned this cartoon, the Fringe was back to celebrating: "We are almost back to pre-Covid levels!". Despite hotels at £500 per night and flats at over ten grand for the month of August, we seem to be back on track, seeking to break records and grow, grow, grow. Where will it end? According to some, it has a divine right to grow forever, and probably will.

Fringe Extremes

The Fringe, with more than 3000 shows on offer, is a place of extremes. On one side there are large scale shows that simply use the Fringe as a stop off point for touring. One advantage for you, the punter, can be that shows that might charge over fifty quid on tour, coming in at more affordable prices during August in Edinburgh. At the other extremes are all the wonderful and crazy experiments that you might only find at the fringe - in a basement of a shop, a graveyard or in a swimming pool. You might find yourself following an augmented reality site specific verbatim theatre piece via a customised app. It's all here. Try imagining something nuts, you might just find it in the Fringe programme.

Fringe Destroying The Planet

This cartoon is a bit too obvious and worthy in its message. It was the first (and last) on I tried making on a tablet computer. An overheard conversation. As the planet dies, many scheme to fly their light entertainment across the globe for more personal glory, reviews, trailing dark smoke out of their arses. Do you really need to fly that show across the world? Many other performers have chosen to stay more local in the name of sustainability. Some still readily fly to other fringes, but where they feel the importance of their work justifies it.

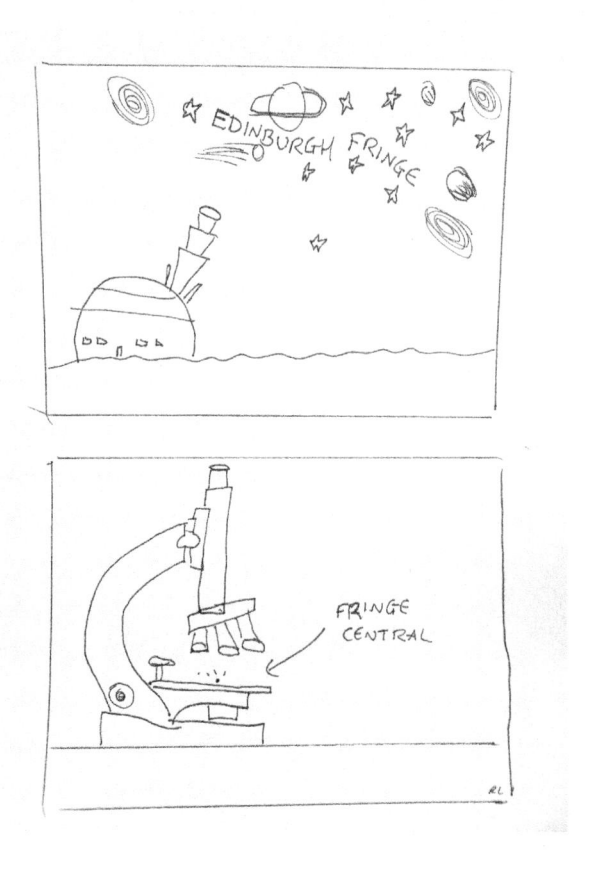

Fringe Central

Another "angry" cartoon. The Fringe Society often likes to trumpet its growth and the fact is it now breaks 3500 shows on a regular basis. It can seem to be fixated on scale and growth and become monstrous in the process. Yet the glory days of the participant hub in Crichton Street seem to have passed and I was saddened in 2023 to see what a tint space was on offer to 3000 plus shows who pay their fair whack for services. A couple of printers and a handful of sofas to share the reviews and chill out? Give me a break. Here's hoping to a much more generous offering in the future as the fringe acquires new buildings.

Free Fringe Ethos

This cartoon feels rather cynical now I look at it again. There was a time when free fringe meant you paid on the way out, if you chose to. Then a few rumours began to circulate that some performers were being rather pushy about money being handed over. Then new models developed where you could pay in advance for a free fringe show to guarantee your seat or your place in a priority queue. It has all got a bit complicated as performers and show makers try to cover at least some of the exorbitant costs of staging a show at the Fringe. But there is a danger the free fringe model could become even more bureaucratic than the "main" pay fringe. So far the vast majority of shows still keep it simple. If you want to, put something in the donations bucket on the way out.

> "An Arthur's Seat of pointless, distractive, energy-sapping mobile phones"

SELFIE!

Dark Fringe View

It is there in the gaps between the tenements. You'll find it hard to walk around a city and not see or feel the looming presence of Arthur's Seat. You will probably climb it at least once if you are a regular fringe goer. Precipices can be places of major decision, inspiration, and of gazing into the abyss. I was supping Scottish Breakfast blend in a cafe near Nicolson Street and there was Arthur's seat, blending with fringers taking selfies. The cartoon arose from an imagination of just how many self images are captured in the grey city in August. I imagined all those phones piled up, as large as Arthur's Seat. Many will be taken at the tip of that looming giant. Yet, if you put the damn gadget down for a moment, and admire the view, feel humbled by the scale and the beauty of this city, you might just notice the vista of possibilities, and your tiny cares might just fly away leaving clearer vision ahead.

"DANCE" | *"PHYSICAL THEATRE"*

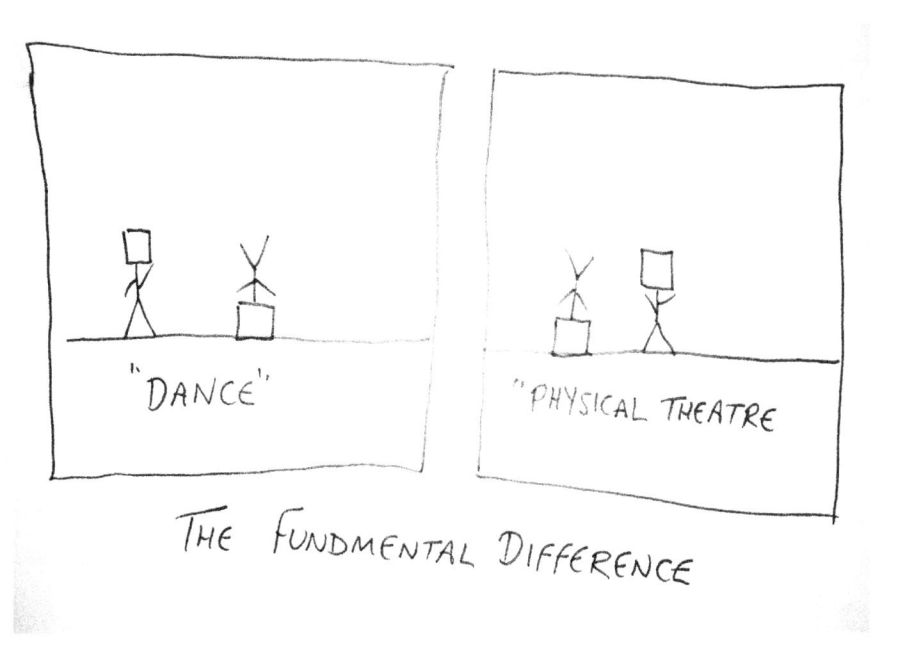

THE FUNDMENTAL DIFFERENCE

Dance Or Physical Theatre

I overheard this conversation at the Fringe that bordered on an argument. "It isn't dance, it's physical theatre!" "No. it's definitely dance - there was music and no one said anything!". The two are lumped together in a single category in the Edfringe programme. Do categories and labels matter? If you like theatre, look in the dance and physical theatre category as well. A lot of solo theatre performers put themselves in the comedy category (the biggest one by far) in the programme because they think they will sell more tickets. There's a risk as lager cans are thrown at your Vladimir and Estragon by drunk, disgruntled comedy show punters.

Climate Disaster And Who Cares

I got angry at the hypocrisy of shows at Edfringe that had flown halfway round the world to be there and shows that flew from Edfringe to fringes all over the globe, just for the fun of it, for the continued fame and power trip. Self-indulgent, grasping and indifferent to the climate change statements on many of their web sites. Climate change becomes the elephant in the room for show makers for whom a heating up planet becomes an annoying inconvenience to their hardly necessary world tour. Grump ongoing on this one. The irony of me being part of it not lost on me.

Fringe Wisdom

wireless connection

Some conversations should be face to face

Wireless Connection At The Fringe

I see people spending most of their fringe not physically present as they pass their time stuck in the digital world. Social media is a poor replacement for the sights, sounds and smells of this, the world's largest and most monstrous arts festival. Look up from your virtual life and enjoy and taste every moment of this crazed and wonderful month in Edinburgh.

7
The Fringe Aftermath

West End Transfer

They had such a beautifully and cleverly crafted set that fitted into their fifty seater venue like a glove. It left me wonderingL what happens if they actually succeed? How is that perfectly sized (for a Quaker meeting house) living room set going to be transferred to a London 400 seater on a bigger stage? Imagine your show playing in different spaces and not just your fringe venue. Be agile and flexible with your imagination. Perish the thought, you might actually sell out and need to take that set on tour!

September

August can be busy busy busy. It was certainly busy back in 2016 when I penned this cartoon. Put those serious about a life after the fringe for their work need to be remembering that the fringe ends in August and you need to have bookings in your calendar so you can hit the ground running straight afterwards. The energy crashes very quickly but creating continuity which involves planning, scheduling, booking, creating and networking in August is like planting seeds that will bloom in the months to follow. And it is the sign that you are not just here for the party but here for the ongoing story.

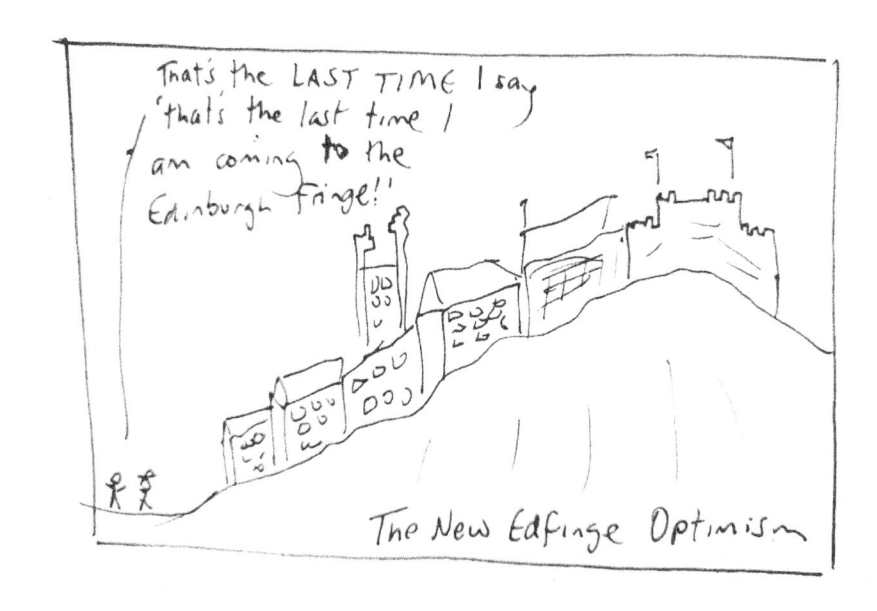

That's the LAST TIME I say, 'that's the last time I am coming to the Edinburgh Fringe!'

The New Edfringe Optimism

Never Again

Admit it. Don't waste your precious energy on this "this is the last time" nonsense. You know you'll be back. Whatever happens, you will play another hand. Or … perhaps a year off, or moving to new and different pastures is the best step you could ever take. This is the great "fringe decision" made each year.

Nevermore

Thus quoth the Raven. The Edinburgh Fringe may be the largest arts festival in the world, but it is not the only one. There really are many other Fringes, right across our dying planet. I know many theatre and arts makers who have never done the Edinburgh Fringe or who came a few times and then decided they needed it no more. They thrive, they tour, they create, they explore, fail and succeed. You do not need to come here. You really do not need to come here.

Keep Coming Back

This cartoon was born of an overheard conversation. Two theatre makers were taking stock and mostly counting the cost of their Fringe. Little, it would seem, had gone right. Empty houses, paltry reviews, a broken crown (of the tooth kind) with an emergency trip to a sadistic dentist. And then the pause, not a very long one, as the conversation turned to what they would do to put these problems right NEXT YEAR! It can, this Fringe thing. It does, this Fringe thing. This Fringe has a pull to it and people return year after year, for another go.

Fringe Connecting

There's a lot of connecting at the Fringe, rooted in the fingortip ephemeral touch of smartphone to smartphone. But those connections are easy to make and easier to then ignore. Deeper and more lasting connections are made in the venue bars, cafes, courtyards and in some genuine eye contact.

8
Fringe in the Age of AI

Fringe And AI

Yes, Ai is here and reviews were already being written with ChatGPT or Claude in 2023. I also just noticed my local Brighton based Argus newspaper now has "AI-assisted" reporters. Check the sources of reviews. If it feels like it has been written by AI, then it probably has. AI can be a useful to assist writing and pressure to get copy out to deadline rises at Edfringe as shows do the whole month less and less. But beware reviews that don't actually describe the show being reviewed, because the reviewer was never physically there.

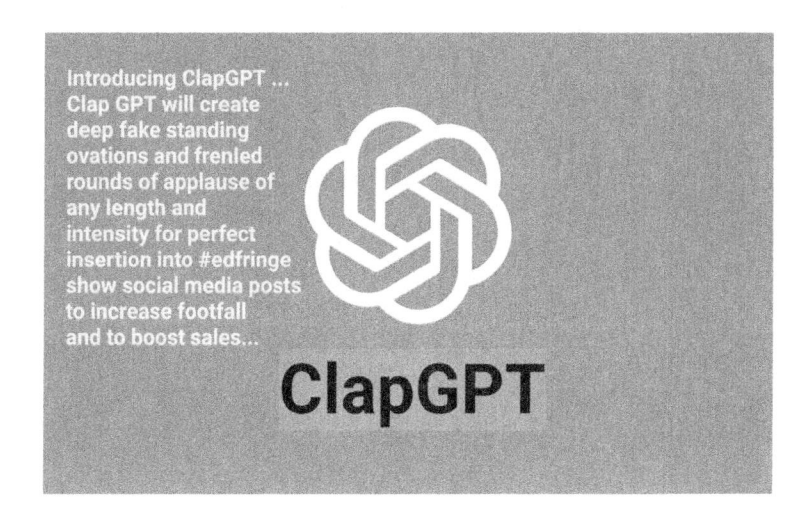

> Introducing ClapGPT ... Clap GPT will create deep fake standing ovations and frenled rounds of applause of any length and intensity for perfect insertion into #edfringe show social media posts to increase footfall and to boost sales...
>
> **ClapGPT**

Clap Gpt App

Canned laughter has been part of the TV comedy scene for years. Fringe shows are increasingly being live streamed, recorded for watching later or using AI in the lighting and sound box. Not sure if it has happened yet but singers have dubbed pretending to be live or often used recorded backing vocals. Soon there will be AI-assisted applause and live canned laughter. I created this cartoon when I saw a video showing the audience reaction to a live comedian on their publicity video. I wasn't sure the audience laughter was the same audience for the show they were selling...

Rise Of AI

This is not really a cartoon about anything specific to the fringe. Appendix coming out of a show about AI in the world. There are a lot of Black Mirror type shows at the fringe these days. Most of the views are pessimistic and try to shock. Most paint a dark view of our digital future. Is there any optimism to be had in the arts world as it tries to explore the rise of AI for audiences?

9
Fringe Craft

SOLO THEATRE:
" I have no need of anyone else..."

Solo Show

Solo work has been on the right year on year at the Fringe, at least partly because, as legend of solo theatre, Pip Utton, once pointed out to me: "The profit share is a lot better". Some solo performers are genuinely at ease in their own company. But bringing a solo show to the fringe can be a lonely and isolating experience. Alone together is the cure, so reach out, guarantee each other's work and get the synergy that comes from joining up at least a bit.

The Edfringe Diet

Yes, there really is a deep fried Mars Bar. Some catering outlets will deep fry anything you take in for the purpose. Whether you are a fringe punter or show maker, if you are in Edinburgh for more than a couple of days, don't kill your chances of a decent length life. Stick a bit of greenery into your daily diet. For month-long performers, look after your health and diet if only because healthy eating may give you better sleep and fringe success over weeks and weeks is all about energy.

Managing Your Money

Money quickly goes on a ten quid gourmet burger or a twelve quid artisan haggis pie. People are often overworked and underpaid (if paid at all). Yes, you do have to budget in Expensiveville, Scotland. There are cheaper joints on the fringes of this fringe and shopping around can keep your pocket from emptying too quickly. Remember there will still be bills on pay in September.

Fixed Formats

It was back in the 2010s that "improv" as a format started to irritate me. I have worked in the field of improvisation on and off for many years. At the Fringe it can all get a bit formulaic and the formats can become repetitive, the very opposite of what improvisation is supposed to be about. Coming back year after year with the same format bothers me. It may or may not bother you. Certainly some improv shows have a loyal audience who come back to see them year after year in their usual time slot with a tried and trusted improv recipe. My advice: keep improvising your improve, right to its core. Keep it vibrant, fresh, surprising everyone, even you.

Venue Noise Bleed

Venues with noise bleed are many and varied at the Fringe. I have heard constantly dripping pipes in a show set in a desert. Buses and police cars hooted outside an intimate two hander set in a yurt with a flapping door. The worst can be a noisy, insensitive usher berating latecomers. Venues at the Fringe are often pop up with soundproofing issues. But even bricks and mortar spaces can be ruined with noisy fans trying to cool down the space from relentless crowds and poor insulation. Check your spaces for noise bleed. Fight for the silence you need.

VR At The Fringe

Virtual reality arrived at the Fringe a few years back. It will only increase in the future. Be ready to put on your head set for the AI-assisted trailer at the start, or make sure your phone is no antique as you are invited to download the immersive reality show app.

The Show Is Still Bedding In

People go into denial at the fringe. They become victims of their own utopian ideals, bought lock stock into their own self-deceiving publicity. Sometimes you have to make changes, admit it isn't going to plan. Be humble, get back into the rehearsal room and set things to rights. You can turn things around at the Fringe, but not if you are all colluding with mediocrity, or worse, collectively labelling crap and honey.

10
The Great Bedtime Grab

Accommodation Costs

Accommodation costs continue to skyrocket in Edinburgh. Staying out of town can be inconvenient but significantly cheaper. Stay on a bus or train route, or on the far side of a lovely park. Staying ten miles out of town can still be feasible and even present an opportunity to get away from the city centre noise. And you can still promote in the locality where you are staying. The bus journey in and out of the city can be a daily rhythm to collect your thoughts, plan or debrief the busy day. Depending on where you are staying, cycling can be a challenge on some roads. Staying out in the Pentland Hills can give you Nature, inspiration and some clean air.

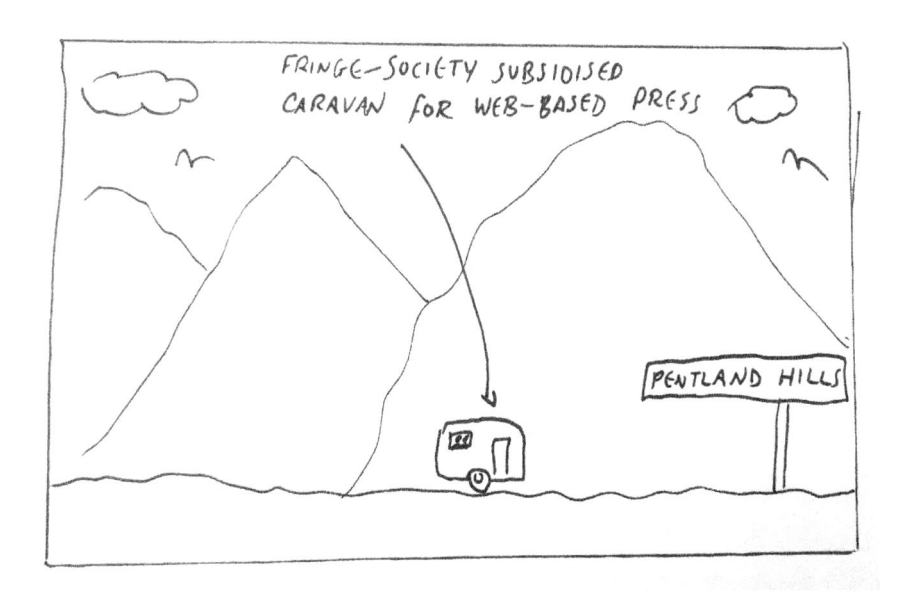

Media Cheap Accommodation

After complaints about accommodation being outrageously costly at the Fringe and genuine evidence that many media outlets and journalists were deserting the Fringe ship, attempts were made by venues and the Fringe Society to offer subsidised affordable accommodation to budget-bereft journos and starving photographers with twelve inch lenses. Some of it, I heard, was rather nice. Some of it was ... well this cartoon was a cynical response on a rainy day at a bus stop.

Out Of Town Accommodation

Many fringe-goers and theatre makers camp at the Fringe, bussing or biking in and out of the city. It can be lovely, it can be beautiful, it can be affordable, it can be cold and wet. A tent, a campervan or a caravan. Viable alternatives to seven grand at a city centre NightNightLodge for three weeks.

11
AI Cartoons

Being too contemporary

Classic plays at the Fringe can be hard to market as there may be half a dozen competing versions of the Macbeth you have brought to Edinburgh. Some are set in modern times and some even in the future or in alternative realities. Some play with the story, some play with the characters, some rewrite the whole script based around one or two characters. If Stoppard did it, so can you. I have seen some terrific modern versions of Shakespeare or Dickens. I have also seen some terrible ones. If you decide to set a classic play in a more contemporary setting there has to be a good reason to do so, it should not feel like a gimmick force fitted. Find the authentic reason if you must mess with it.

Being too niche

Audiences simply do not get some shows and that can quickly lead to a very few people going to them. If your show is very niche or unique make sure you've still explained it properly to potential punters. Every show has its audience but not every audience is at the Fringe.

Deep fake fringe

This was the first cartoon I created using generative AI. Though this technology is pretty incredible I am happy to head back to my physical paper and pen. But we cannot get away from the fact that AI is now here, and already some fairly familiar sounding famous voices have been deep faked by AI voiceovers to save money. Be clear about your reasons for using this exciting and scary technology and make sure you use it well.

"OH, DRONE-EO, DRONE-EO, WHEREFORE ART THOU, DRONE-EO?"

Drone promos

I thought the drone was following me through the Meadows, but it was actually following a stand-up comedian who was going to use the footage in her show or perhaps in a trailer. Drones can allow you a bit of outside broadcasting or a slow close-up to a bedroom just like in a Hollywood Movie. Drone filming creates all kinds of possibilities for fringe shows that want to make use of film. Or you could just use it to check the people you are paying to flyer your show are actually doing their job…

Procrastination at the fringe

Procrastination has a lot going for it. You don't have to come every year to the Fringe just because you're trapped in the cycle of repetition or fringe addiction. Think it through and be very open to the idea that you might take a year off. I have met many performers and theatre makers who are glad that that year or two out, allowed them to refresh, rethink and re-emerge.

Draw Your Own Cartoon
Go On give it a go, while the muse is with you.

Draw Your Own Cartoon

Go On give it a go, while the muse is with you.

Draw Your Own Cartoon
Go On give it a go, while the muse is with you.

Printed in Great Britain
by Amazon